CHEW, CHEW, GULP!

LAUREN THOMPSON

illustrated by
JARRETT J. KROSOCZKA

Mc Graw Hill Education

mhreadingwonders.com

Text copyright ©2011 by Lauren Thompson.

Illustrations copyright ©2011 by Jarrett J. Krosoczka.

Reprinted by arrangement with Margaret K. McElderry Books, an imprint of Simon & Schuster Children's Publishing Division. All rights reserved.

No part of this publication may be reproduced or distributed in any form or by any means, or stored in a database or retrieval system, without the prior written consent of McGraw-Hill Education, including, but not limited to, network storage or transmission, or broadcast for distance learning.

Send all inquiries to:
McGraw-Hill Education
Two Penn Plaza
New York NY 10121

ISBN: 978-0-07-678449-3
MHID: 0-07-678449-5

Printed in the United States of America

5 6 7 8 9 MER 25 24 23 22 21

To Joy C.
—L. T.

For Joyce and Greg,
who keep me well fed
—J. J. K.

Eating isn't hard to do.

Follow us!
We'll show you.

Curl it.

SPAGHETTI

Scoop it.

Loop it.

Prod it.

TOMATO

Pop it.

Chew, chew,

GULP!

Sip it.

MILK

Nip it.

Pick it.

GRAPES

Lick it.

ICE CREAM CONE

Nibble it.

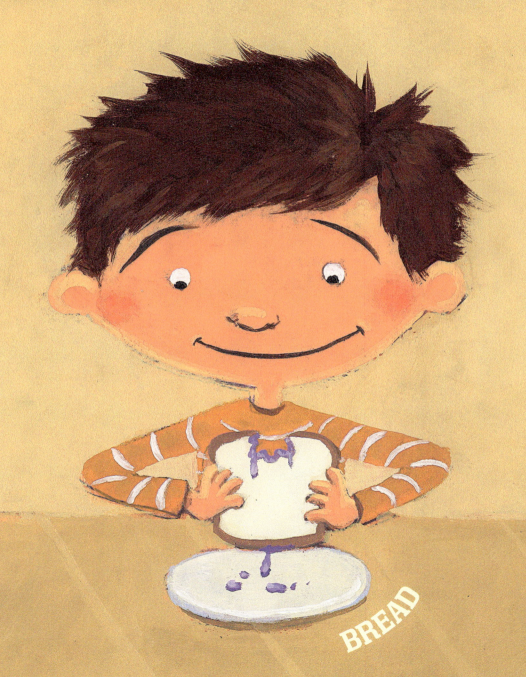

Crumble it.

COOKIES

Jab, jab,

POKE!

Munch it.

APPLE

Crunch it.

CARROT

Chomp it.

CORN ON THE COB

Chop it.

Gobble it.

Guzzle it.

Slurp, **slurp,**

Easy as pie!

Now YOU try!